TASTE!

Our Family Recipes

ANN JOHNSON

With Best Selling Author

SHARI W. QUINN

Published by Shari Quinn Publishing

Taste! is a collection of family recipes. Any resemblance to any other recipes is entirely coincidental.

Available on Kindle and other retail outlets

To order additional copies of this title, contact your favorite bookstore or visit www.shariquinn.com or email: info@shariquinn.com

Cover Design by Sterling A. McCollum

Cover Image by Arthur Danzy, 2015

Shari's hair by Jade Lewis-Gibson, Jade's Hair Envy, Albany, NY

Edited by Shari W. Quinn
Interior Design by Shari W. Quinn

Printed in the United States of America
CreateSpace, Charleston, SC

ISBN: 0692576320
ISBN-13: 978-0692576328 (Shari Quinn Publishing)

To our family,

It is our greatest joy that we share and preserve the generations of our treasured family's favorite recipes and the flavors of our Alabama family roots. We hope you continue to enjoy these meals and traditions, and pass them along to the generations to come.

From our kitchen to yours!

All our love,

Shari & Ann

In my South, the most
treasured things
passed down from
generation to
generation are the
family recipes.

Robert St. John

Other Books
by Shari Quinn Publishing

Disloyalty

42 Strategies to Market Your Book:
An Author's Guide

CONTENTS

Acknowledgements

We would like to thank our family for their unwavering support and enthusiasm throughout this project. We would also like to thank the many contributors of the family recipes and those whose recipes inspired us including Ms. Willie B. Quinn, Aunt Marie, Aunt Katie, McKinley (Kenny) Johnson, Nina Faye Marbury, Gloria Jeffries, Lovie Jean Barnes and LaQuanda Lawson.

In this cookbook, we also pay tribute to those whose amazing recipes have equally inspired us and touched our hearts, the late Barbara Johnson Shephard (Ann's mother and Shari's aunt), Aunt Margaret, Uncle Jesse, Aunt Mattie Mae, Uncle CH, and our late cousins Pearlie Mae Hamilton Bardwell and Gaye Nell Black. May their memories live forever.

We hope this cookbook inspires everyone to preserve their family recipes as it is greatest inheritance you can ever leave.

Prelude

Being the fourth oldest child in my family, I did not have the chore of cooking as my older siblings. When I got married I could cook the basics - fried chicken, pork chops and French fries but not the typical Sunday dinners known to African American families. So I am a self-taught cook, having learned by observing my mother, aunts and mother-in-law and calling my mother to ask how to cook a particular dish. I have always loved to bake and loved following desert recipes that was not the norm in my traditional southern African American family who typically cooked by sight not measurements. I soon became a Sunday Dinner cook often having numerous family members and guests over on Sundays and all holidays.

Ann Johnson

Appetizers and Dips

I sustain myself with the love of family

Maya Angelou

Homemade Healthy Granola Bars

From Shari's kitchen

¼ cup walnuts, chopped
2 ½ cups of oats (I split with granola)
1 cup seeds (flaxseeds, sunflower seeds, pumpkin seeds - I like to mix them up.)
½ cup dried cranberries
½ cup agave nectar (or honey)
1 teaspoon ground cinnamon
¾ cup peanut butter (I use almond butter)

1. Toast oats, granola and walnuts on 350 degrees for 10 minutes
2. Mix in a bowl with cinnamon, seeds and dried cranberries
3. Mix agave nectar (or honey), peanut butter (or almond butter) in separate bowl, microwave for 20 seconds.
4. Pour over oat mixture and fold with spatula or spoon.

5. Line cookie sheet with wax paper. Pour mixture into cookie sheet, press down with spatula.
6. Cover with foil or saran wrap and put in the fridge for 1-2 hours to prevent from crumbling. When ready to cut, use a pizza cutter to also prevent crumbling.

Optional: Use apricots or other dried fruits to the mixture. You can add other natural dried fruits of your liking. You can also add shredded coconut and chocolate morsels. It's best to get all of these items from your local Fresh Market or Whole Foods. It'll be a little pricey but this recipe will yield several batches so you'll get your money's worth and eat a healthy snack.

Pineapple Meatballs

From Shari's kitchen

1 cup brown sugar

3 teaspoons cornstarch

1 ¾ pineapple juice

¼ white vinegar

1 ½ tablespoon soy sauce

1 ½ teaspoon Worcesterchire sauce

14 ounce can pineapples, cut up

1. Mix all ingredients together. Simmer in a large sauce pan on stove.
2. Pour over meatballs and heat. Bring to a boil, and reduce heat to simmer.

Buffalo Chicken Dip
From Shari's kitchen

1 (8 oz.) cream cheese, softened
½ cup Franks Red Hot Buffalo Wing Sauce
½ cup Bleu Cheese dressing
2 cups Shredded cooked chicken
1 container (about 1-1 ½ cups) crumbled bleu cheese
Handful of shredded cheddar cheese

Combine all ingredients in baking dish, bake at 350 for 20 minutes. 5 minutes before finishing baking, top with shredded cheese and finish baking.

Crockpot instructions: Combine all ingredients, pour in crockpot, cook on low for 3 hours. Before finish, top with shredded cheese.

Serve with tortilla chips, crackers or vegetables.

Cheese Onion Dip

A favorite from Ann's kitchen

1 cup chopped onion

1 cup mayo

1 cup sharp shredded cheese

Mix well and heat in microwave until cheese melts. Serve with crackers.

Homemade Guacamole
From Shari's kitchen

3 avocados
4 garlic cloves, pressed or minced
½ medium onion, chopped
1 medium tomato
¼ tsp. chopped cilantro
Juice of one lime
Pinch of salt
Dash of black pepper
1 jalapeno pepper, finely chopped and seeded

Slice the avocados in half. Remove the pit with a spoon and scoop the avocado out into a bowl.

Squeeze lime juice in a bowl, add salt and pepper to lime juice. Add jalapeno, tomatoes onion and cilantro. Mix in avocados.

Using fork, mash together to desired consistency.

Serve with tortilla chips or use as a spread.

Beer Dip

From Shari's kitchen

2 (8 ounces) packages cream cheese, softened

1 (1 ounce) package ranch dressing mix

2 cups shredded Cheddar cheese

1/3 cup beer

In a medium bowl, combine cream cheese and dressing mix. Stir in cheddar cheese and add beer. The mixture will appear mushy. Cover bowl and set in refrigerator for 3 hours or preferably overnight.

Shrimp Log

From Ann's kitchen

This is easy to make, spread is delicious on crackers as a hors d'oeuvre.

8 oz. cream cheese, softened

1 can small shrimp

Cocktail sauce

Parsley

In a bowl, mix softened cream cheese and shrimp until well blended. On a serving dish, shape mixture into a log and chill. Just before serving, pour cocktail sauce over log and garnish with parsley.

Hot Crab Dip

From Ann's kitchen

1 8 oz. cream cheese
½ cup shredded cheddar cheese
1 lb. crab (or imitation)
¾ cup light sour cream
2 tablespoons lemon juice
1 tsp. Worcestershire sauce
¾ tsp. dry mustard
¼ tsp. garlic powder

Combine all ingredients except crab and cheese. Cream together, add crab and cheese. Spray pan then pour ingredients. Bake for 325 for 30 minutes.

Ultimate Party Meatballs

From Ann's kitchen

1-16 oz. can jellied cranberry sauce
1-12 oz. bottle Chili sauce
1-2 pound bag frozen, pre-cooked, cocktail-size meatballs

Combine sauces in a large saucepan. Cook over medium-low heat, stirring until smooth. Add meatballs. Cover and cook for 15 minutes or until meatballs are heated through, stirring occasionally. Makes 30 appetizer servings.

Slow Cooker Preparation: Place meatballs in a slow cooker. Combine sauces and pour over meatballs. Cover and cook 4 hours on high.

Homemade Cocktail Meatballs

From Ann's kitchen

4 lbs. ground beef

3 eggs (slightly beaten)

Minced onions

Bread crumbs

Salt & Pepper

1-12 oz. bottle chili sauce

1-12 oz. jar grape jelly

Dash of lemon juice

Blend first 5 ingredients; roll into small balls and fry or bake in oven. Combine chili sauce, grape jelly and lemon juice. Simmer a couple of hours.

Sweet and Sour Meatballs

From Ann's kitchen

(2) 15 ounce can tomato sauce

½ cup light brown sugar

½ cup Chile sauce

3 tablespoons red wine vinegar

1 tablespoon Worcestershire sauce

Mix all ingredients, pour mixture over meatballs and heat.

Add 1-2 lbs. bag of meatballs.

Brandy Meatballs

From Shari's kitchen

⅓ cup brandy

½ cup ketchup

1 tablespoon dried onion

1 cup BBQ sauce

½ cup water

Mix all ingredients together. Pour mixture over meatballs and heat.

Coconut Macaroon

From Ann's kitchen

6 cups sweetened shredded coconut flakes

1-14 oz. can sweetened condensed milk

2 teaspoons vanilla extract

Preheat oven to 350 degrees. In large bowl, stir together coconut flakes, sweetened condensed milk and vanilla until well combined. Use a small spoon to scoop out roughly 3 tablespoons of the mixture to form small mounds, spaced about 2 inches apart on a parchment paper-lined baking sheet. Bake for 12-18 minutes until the tops are golden brown and the macaroons are desired level of crispness.

Fruit Yogurt Dip
From Ann's kitchen

1 cup nonfat plain yogurt

1 tablespoon honey

¼ teaspoon ground cinnamon

1. In a medium bowl, combine all ingredients
2. Mix well

Note: Do not add honey if using vanilla yogurt; serve with fruit.

Monkey Bread

From Shari's kitchen

¾ cup granulated sugar
2 teaspoons ground cinnamon
4 cans refrigerated biscuits
½ cup butter or margarine, melted
¾ cup packed brown sugar

Grease or spray Bundt pan

Mix granulated sugar and cinnamon in 1-gallon freezer bag. Cut each biscuit into quarters. Shake quarters in bag to coat; place in pan. Mix butter and brown sugar; pour over biscuit pieces.

Bake at 350 for 40 to 45 minutes or until golden brown. Cool 5 minutes, turn upside down. Serve warm.

Breakfast

Love your family.
Spend time, be kind and serve one another.
Make no room for regrets.
Tomorrow is not promised and today is short.

-Unknown

Mother's Homemade Pancakes

From the kitchen of Shari's mom, Willie B. Quinn

Preheat griddle or skillet

2 cups flour
1 egg
1 cup milk
⅓ cup oil
1 teaspoon salt
3 teaspoons baking powder
¼ cup sugar

Use a ¼ measuring cup to scoop batter to make uniform pancakes. Cook on each side until golden brown.

I love to brush griddle or skillet with Butter flavored Crisco. You can also use vegetable or olive oil.

Serve with hot maple syrup or fresh fruit topping.

Tip: Great with a cap full of vanilla extract.

Sausage and Egg Casserole

From Shari's kitchen

12 eggs
¾ cup half and half
½ teaspoon crushed red pepper flakes
½ teaspoon ground pepper
1 cup shredded cheddar cheese
1 cup shredded Colby cheese
½ cup chopped onion
1 bag (20 oz.) refrigerated cooked shredded hash brown potatoes
1lb bulk sausage, cooked, drained
½ cup chopped roasted red pepper or chopped red bell pepper

In medium bowl, beat eggs, half and half, pepper flakes, salt and pepper with whisk. Reserve ¾ cup cheddar cheese and 2 tablespoons onions; set aside. In small bowl, stir together remaining cheeses.

Layer half of the potatoes, sausage, roasted peppers, remaining onions and cheese in slow cooker or large casserole dish (or baking dish). Repeat layers. Pour eggs mixture over layers.

Slow cooker directions: Cook on low heat setting 4 to 5 hours or on high heat setting for 2 ½ to 3 hours.

Baking dish directions: Bake at 350 for 45 minutes. Sprinkle reserved cheese and onions over top of casserole. Cover; cook 10 minutes longer or until cheese is melted. (Only 5 minutes if in oven).

Hash Brown Creamy Casserole

From Shari's kitchen

2 lbs. frozen hash browns (26-32 ounce bag)
½ cup margarine or butter, melted
1 (10 ¼ ounce) can cream of chicken soup
1 8 oz. container sour cream
½ cup onion, chopped fine
2 cups cheddar cheese, grated or shredded
¼ teaspoon sea salt
¼ teaspoon pepper

Preheat oven to 350 degrees and spray an 11x14 baking dish with cooking spray.

Mix the above ingredients together in a large bowl. Place in prepared pan and bake for 45 minutes or until brown on top.

Alternative: Cook in crockpot on high setting for 3 hours; or 4-5 hours on low setting. Use crockpot liner for easy cleaning. Spray the liner. The casserole should be crispy on the sides and bubbly throughout.

Coconut Pancakes

From Shari's kitchen

2 cups all-purpose flour
½ cup sugar
4 teaspoons baking powder
1 teaspoon salt
½ cup flaked coconut
1-13.5 oz. can coconut milk
4 eggs
¼ cup canola oil
½ teaspoon coconut extract

Sift flour, baking powder and salt into large bowl. Mix in flaked coconut. Beat coconut milk, eggs, oil and extract together.

Add liquid ingredients, mix until combined.

Pour ¼ cup – ½ cup batter on greased and preheated griddle (375 degrees) or skillet.

French Toast Casserole

From Shari's kitchen

1 loaf Italian or French bread, broken in pieces
6 eggs, beaten
1 ½ cup half and half
½ cup sugar
1 tsp. vanilla
½ tsp. cinnamon
1 stick butter, softened
½ cup brown sugar
½ cup chopped nuts (pecans or walnuts)
1 tsp. light karo syrup
Hot syrup

Preheat oven to 350, spray 9x13 baking pan

Add bread pieces to pan; mix eggs, half and half, sugar, vanilla and cinnamon in a separate bowl and pour over bread.

Mix butter, brown sugar, nuts and karo syrup. Spread over bread and egg mixture.

Bake 40 minutes and serve with hot syrup.

Home Fries
From Shari's kitchen

4 potatoes, cut into cubes (leave skin on)
½ onion, sliced thick
½ green pepper
2 tablespoons olive oil
2 cloves of fresh pressed garlic
1 teaspoon of paprika
sprinkle sea salt and pepper

Toss all ingredients into a large bowl. Pour into generously greased baking dish. Bake at 400 degrees for 1 hour to 1½ hours until tender.

Can also be served as dinner item.

Salmon Croquettes

From Shari's kitchen

1 can pink salmon (drained)
1 egg
½ chopped onion
1 tablespoon mustard
Salt, pepper and garlic
2 cups of flour

Heat skillet on medium heat, coat skillet with oil. Mix all ingredients together with 1 tablespoon of flour.

Spoon scoop of mixture into hand, form into ball then press into patties (repeat). Coat both sides of patties with flour. Places patties into hot oil and cook each side for 3-4 minutes or until golden. Do not overcook.

I love to serve with spicy mustard.

Breads and Biscuits

Family is the most important thing in the world.

Princess Diana

Aunt Marie's Broccoli Cornbread

From the kitchen of our Aunt Anne Marie Brace
Durham, NC

This is a family favorite and always requested

10 oz. frozen broccoli, thawed
2 boxes Jiffy corn mix
1 cup cottage cheese
½ chopped onion
4 eggs
2 sticks butter, melted

Optional: Add ½ cup shredded cheddar cheese

Mix all ingredients together, except broccoli. Once mixed, fold thawed broccoli (and optional cheese) into mixture. Pour mixture into greased baking dish.

Bake at 350 degrees for 45 minutes.

Jalapeno Cornbread
From Shari's kitchen

1 ½ cups buttermilk cornbread mix
1 cup all-purpose flour
1 ½ cups milk
4 tablespoons vegetable oil
3 large eggs, beaten
3 teaspoons baking powder
1 cup chopped onion
3 tablespoons sugar
½ teaspoons salt
½ cup cream style corn or fiesta-style corn
½ cup finely chopped jalapeno peppers
1 ½ cups Mexican blend cheese or Pepper Jack (or mix ½ of both), shredded

Preheat oven to 375 degrees. Lightly grease a 9 inch square baking dish and spray with pan spray.

Combine cornbread mix and milk in a mixing bowl. Add remaining ingredients and mix to blend thoroughly.

Pour into three greased 8-inch square baking pans, or one 9x13x2-inch baking pan and one 8-inch square baking pan.

Bake at 350 degrees for 35-40 minutes.

Optional: Add 6 slices of cooked and chopped bacon. Great with chili or baked macaroni and cheese.

Crackling Corn Bread

2 cups white cornmeal
¼ cup sifted all-purpose flour
1 tablespoon sugar
½ teaspoon salt
4 teaspoon salt
1 ½ cups plus 2 tablespoons milk
2 large eggs, beaten well
2 tablespoon (1/4 stick) butter, melted
¼ pound crisp crackling, broken into 1/2-inch pieces

Crackling can be found in Latino grocery store, Cicharones in Spanish

Preheat oven to 350. Grease an 8x8x2-inch pan

Mix dry ingredients; stir in milk and eggs. Pour in butter and cracklings. Pour mixture into pan and bake for 1 hour or until brown and firm.

Zucchini Bread

From Shari's kitchen

This tastes similar to cake - absolutely delicious!

3 eggs
1 cup oil
1 tablespoon grated orange rind
2 cups shredded zucchini
2 cups sugar
¾ cups orange juice
3 ½ cups flour
½ teaspoon salt
1 ½ teaspoon baking powder
½ teaspoon baking soda
1 cup coconut

Blend ingredients together. Fold in zucchini and coconut with spatula. Pour into 2 well-greased and floured bread pans.

Bake at 350 degrees for 1 hour.

7-up Biscuits
From Ann's kitchen

4 cups Bisquick
1 cup sour cream
1 cup 7-Up
½ cup melted butter

Mix Bisquick, sour cream and 7-Up. Dough will be soft - don't worry. Knead and fold dough until coated with your baking mix. Pat dough out and cut biscuits with a round biscuit / cookie cutter. Melt butter in bottom of cookie sheet pan or a 9x13 casserole dish. Place biscuits on top of melted butter and bake at 425 degrees for 12-15 minutes or until brown.

Strawberry Bread

From Ann's kitchen

3 Cups All Purpose Flour
2 Cups Sugar
1 TBSP Ground Cinnamon
1 Tsp Baking Soda
1 Tsp Salt
1 ¼ Cups Vegetable Oil
4 Eggs, Slightly Beaten
2 Cups Sliced Fresh Strawberries
1 ¼ Cups Chopped Walnuts, Optional

In large bowl combine flour, sugar, cinnamon, baking soda and salt. Stir in oil and eggs just until dry ingredients are moistened. Stir in strawberries and, if desired, walnuts. Spoon batter into 2 lightly greased 9x5-inch loaf pans. Bake at 350 degrees for 45 minutes or until done. Makes 2 medium loaves.

Cheese Biscuits
From Ann's kitchen

½ cup shortening
2 cups all-purpose flour
1 tablespoon sugar
2 teaspoons baking powder
¼ teaspoon baking soda
1 teaspoon salt
1/3 cup shredded cheese
¾ cup buttermilk

Heat oven to 450 degrees. Cut shortening into flour, sugar, baking powder, baking soda and salt with pastry blender until mixture resembles fine crumbs. Stir in cheese and buttermilk until dough leaves side of bowl (dough will be soft and sticky).

Turn dough onto lightly floured surface. Knead about 10 times. Roll or pat ½-inch thick. Cut with floured 2 ½- inch round cutters. Place on ungreased cookie sheet about 1-inch apart. Bake until golden brown, about 10 to 12 minutes. Immediately remove from cookie sheet.

Makes 1 dozen biscuits.

Nana Bread

From Ann's kitchen

2 cups flour
1 teaspoon baking soda
½ teaspoon salt
½ cup shortening
¾ cup sugar
2 well-beaten eggs
3 crushed ripe bananas
¼ cup chopped walnuts or pecans

Sift together the flour, soda and salt. In a separate bowl, cream together the rest of the ingredients and then slowly add the dry, sifted ingredients.

Spoon into greased small loaf pans and bake at 325 degrees for 45 minutes. Make sure the center is done by testing with toothpick.

Virginia Cornbread

From Ann's kitchen

2 cups self-rising cornmeal
1 cup all-purpose flour
1 tablespoon baking powder
1 teaspoon baking soda
½ teaspoon salt
2 eggs
1 ½ cups buttermilk

Preheat oven to 325 degrees. Grease an 8x8-inch baking pan. Combine dry ingredients. In a separate bowl, combine eggs and buttermilk. Add liquid ingredients to dry; stir just until mixed. Pour batter into prepared baking pan. Bake at 325 degree oven about 20 minutes or until a toothpick inserted in the center comes out clean. Makes 16 servings.

Note: If self-rising cornmeal is not available in your area, substitute regular yellow cornmeal and increase baking powder to 1 ½ tablespoons and salt to 1 teaspoon.

Pork and Bean Bread

From Ann's kitchen

1 cup boiling water
1 cup raisins
3 eggs
1 cup oil
2 cups sugar
1-16 oz. can pork and beans
3 cups flour
1 teaspoon baking soda
½ teaspoon baking powder
1 teaspoon cinnamon
½ teaspoon salt
1 teaspoon vanilla
1 cup chopped nuts

Pour boiling water over raisins and set aside. Beat together the eggs, oil and sugar. Add the pork and beans and beat well to break up the beans. Sift together the flour, baking soda, baking powder, cinnamon and salt. Add dry ingredients to egg mixture and mix well. Stir in vanilla and nuts. Drain raisins and add to the batter. Mix well and pour into two well-greased loaf pans. Bake in a preheated 325 degrees oven 40-50 minutes until done. Cool 10 minutes on rack and remove from pans. (Bread freezes well.) Makes 2 loaves, 16 slices each.

Note: This unusual bread is sure to surprise and delight those who try it. Pork and beans can be substituted with vegetarian baked beans.

Blueberry Muffins

From the kitchen of Willie B. Quinn, Shari's mom

2 ½ cups of all-purpose flour
¾ cup granulated sugar
1 tablespoon baking powder
½ teaspoon salt
1 pinch ground cinnamon
6 tablespoons unsalted butter, melted
¾ cup milk
2 eggs
2 cups fresh or frozen blueberries (fresh is better)

Grease muffin pan or line with baking cups. Preheat oven to 375 degrees.

Mix flour, sugar, baking powder, salt and cinnamon by hand or fork in a medium bowl.

In a small bowl, whisk together melted butter, milk and eggs. Add liquid mixture to dry mixture and mix gently. Fold in blueberries.

Pour batter into greased muffin pan. Bake 20 to 25 minutes.

Lemon Muffins

From the kitchen of Willie B. Quinn, Shari's' mom

6 cups all-purpose flour
2 tablespoons baking powder
1 ½ teaspoons salt
1 pound butter, softened
4 cups sugar
8 eggs
2 cups milk
Grated zest of 4 lemons
Juice of 2 lemons
6 cups confectioners' sugar
Hot water
1 tablespoon butter

Heat oven to 350 degrees. Butter and flour large muffin pans or use baking cups.

Combine flour, baking powder and salt in a large bowl. Cream butter and sugar in a food processor. Add eggs, one at a time. Stop processor and add the milk. Scrape the sides of the bowl, replace lid and mix until blended. Add the lemon rind into the butter mixture.

Add in the dry ingredients but mix until blended. Fill muffin pan and bake 20 minutes or until inserted toothpick comes out clean.

Combine lemon juice, 5 cups confectioners' sugar and butter in a small bowl. Add remaining confectioners' sugar and hot water to adjust thickness to the desired consistency. Dip cool muffins in icing.

Hush Puppies

From Ann's kitchen

2 cups self-rising cornmeal
½ cup flour
1 teaspoon sugar
1 medium onion, chopped
3 eggs
¾ cup milk
Vegetable oil for deep-frying

Combine the dry ingredients with the onion. Mix in the eggs and milk to make sticky dough. Drop by tablespoon into deep hot oil.

Serve with fish.

Homemade Pie Crust

From the kitchen of Willie B. Quinn, Shari's mom

2 cups flour
1 teaspoon salt
¾ cup Crisco
5 tablespoons cold water

Blend flour and salt in large bowl. Cut shortening into flour mixture with pastry blender or fork until coarse crumbs form. Stir in enough water with fork until dough holds together.

Divide dough in half. Shape into 1/2 -inch discs. Wrap in plastic wrap. Chill in refrigerator for 30 minutes.

Roll out each disc 2 inches larger than pie plate on floured surface.

Buttermilk Biscuits

From the kitchen of Willie B. Quinn, Shari's mom

2 cups flour
2 teaspoons baking powder (double acting)
½ teaspoon salt
1/3 cup Crisco
1 cup buttermilk (or regular milk)

Preheat oven to 450. Sift dry ingredients together; cut in shortening until mixture resembles coarse meal. Quickly stir in buttermilk. Knead dough lightly; roll to 1/2 -inch thickness on lightly floured surface.

Cut in 2-inch rounds. Although you can use a cookie cutter, my mom always used a rim-floured water glass.

Place on ungreased baking sheet. Bake 13 to 15 minutes. Makes a dozen plus biscuits.

Main Dishes

Some of the most important conversations I've ever had occurred at my family's dinner table.

Bob Ehrlich

Swiss Chicken

From Shari's kitchen

This is a favorite that my cousins LaQuanda and Nicole Lawson always asks me to make. I've only made it for them once or twice over 15 years ago but they haven't stopped asking me to make it again so this recipe is for them.

6 skinless, boneless chicken breast halves
6 slices Swiss cheese
1 (10.75) can condensed cream of chicken soup
¼ cup milk
1 (8 ounce) package dry Italian bread crumbs
½ cup melted butter

Preheat oven to 350 degrees. Lightly grease a 9x13 inch baking dish.

Arrange chicken breasts in a baking dish. Place one slice of Swiss cheese on top of each chicken breast. Combine cream of chicken soup and milk in a medium bowl, and pour over chicken breasts. Sprinkle with bread crumbs. Pour melted butter over top, and cover with foil. Bake 50 minutes or until chicken is no longer pink and juices run clear.

Uncles Jesse's Boston Butt

From the kitchen of our awesome late uncle, Jesse Frank Hall

This is not his original recipe but we tried our best duplicate it through the direction of our aunt Anne Marie Brace.

(1) 5-pound Pork roast or Boston butt

Mix seasonings to make dry rub:

- 2 teaspoons smoked paprika
- 2 teaspoons garlic powder
- 2 teaspoons onion power
- 2 teaspoons cumin
- 1 teaspoon cayenne Pepper
- 2 teaspoons salt
- 1-½ teaspoons black pepper
- 1 teaspoons white pepper (optional)

Preheat oven to 350; Wash Boston Butt and pat dry.

Blend dry ingredients; rub olive oil on meat; and generously rub mixture on oiled meat. Bake at 350°F degrees for 2 ½ to 3 hours. Generally 60-90 minutes for every pound. Half way, turn the roast to ensure even cooking.

Turn oven off and cover Boston Butt with foil and let stand for 20 minutes. Slice and serve.

Grill method (preferred): Place on covered grill or smoker for 2 hours.

Leftover Thanksgiving Turkey Quiche

From Shari's kitchen

1 cup shredded cheddar cheese (preferably aged - I also like to use pepper jack)
1 (9 inch) frozen deep dish pie shell, thawed
1 cup shredded or diced leftover turkey or chicken
⅓ cup diced roasted red pepper
2 green or white onions, thinly sliced
¾ cup heavy cream
1 tablespoon all-purpose flour
3 eggs
1 ¼ teaspoon salt

Preheat oven to 375 degrees; bake shell for 5 minutes

Sprinkle cheese in bottom of pie shell. Add turkey, roasted red peppers and onions, using fork toss gently to combine and spread evenly.

In a medium bowl, whisk together cream and flour. Add eggs and salt, and whisk until well combined. Slowly pour over cheese mixture, using fork to allow cream mixture to fill pie shell evenly. Place on cookie sheet to catch overspill while baking. Bake on bottom rack for about 45 minutes or until top is golden, edges puff and knife inserted in center comes out clean. (Optional: sprinkle top with additional shredded cheese before baking). Let cool 10 minutes before cutting into wedges.

Chicken Pot Pie

From Ann's kitchen

2 Ready bake pie crust shells

Filing:

1 bag frozen mixed vegetables
1 can of cream of chicken soup
2 ½ cups cooked chicken
⅓ onion, chopped
salt and pepper to taste
2 tablespoons olive

1. In large skillet, add olive oil and sauté onions for 2 minutes. Add chopped chicken breasts and brown.
2. Mix all ingredients together in a sauce pan.
3. In 9" inch pie dish, layer pie shell into dish
4. Add chicken to mixture and pour mixture into shell
5. Cover with 2nd pie shell and seal edges with fork. Cut 4-6 slits on top crust.
6. Bake at 350 degrees for 45 minutes or until golden brown.
7. Let stand 5 minutes before serving.

Shari's Amore Pasta Sauce & Meatballs with Fettuccine

1 (28 oz.) can crushed tomatoes
1 (28 oz.) can diced tomatoes
1 (6 0z.) tomato paste
1 bay leaf
1 large onion, sliced thick
3 garlic cloves
1 tsp. parsley
2 tsp. oregano
1 ½ tsp. garlic
Sea salt (about 15 turns) & ¾ tsp. black pepper
4-5 tablespoons sugar
1 tsp. Mrs. Dash Original Table Blend
½ tsp. Mrs. Dash Garlic & Herb Blend
a splash of red wine (optional)

In a large pan, coat bottom with olive oil, sauté onions and pressed or minced garlic over medium heat, don't let onions or garlic brown; add cans of tomatoes and paste, add bay leaf and seasonings. Bring to a boil and reduce to simmer for 45-60 minutes covered, occasionally stir.

Serve with Shari's Amore Homemade Meatballs
(see next page)

Shari's Amore Homemade Meatballs

2 lbs. ground turkey (I prefer to use fresh meatloaf mix from the Italian grocery store)
1 envelope packet of McCormick's meatball seasoning
2 eggs, beaten
1/8 cup milk
¼ cup breadcrumbs
¼ cup grated parmesan cheese
1 tsp. garlic, sea salt and pepper
¼ cup homemade pasta sauce from above

Mix together with your hands (I use gloves because I hate getting my hands messy).

In a casserole or large baking dish, spray pan and coat with homemade pasta sauce. Use a small cookie scooper to make uniform balls. Place meatballs in pan and bake uncovered for 45-60 minutes. I usually end up with 3 pans.

Makes approx. 3 dozen meatballs

Serve meatballs and pasta sauce over al dente Fettuccine

Shrimp Scampi with Orzo

From the kitchen of Gloria Jeffries, Ann's sister
Childersburg, AL

8 ounces Orzo pasta (about 2 cups)
2 shallots, chopped
5 cups (6 ounces) Fresh Arugula
2 tablespoons olive oil
1 lb. shrimp, cleaned and deveined
½ cup dry white wine

1. Boil orzo as directed on package.
2. In large skillet coat with olive oil, place shallots and cook until soft (2-3 minutes), add shrimp and cook until pink (2-3 minutes). Remove shrimp from the skillet. Increase heat to high. Add the wine and arugula. Stir and make sure bottom of skillet doesn't burn. Cook for 1 minute until most of the wine has evaporated and the arugula ha wilted.
3. Sprinkle with salt and pepper.
4. Make vinaigrette (see next page).
5. Pour orzo in skillet with shrimp, shallots and arugula; add vinaigrette. Mix well and enjoy!

Continued on next page

Vinaigrette Dressing:

2 lemons
½ cup extra virgin olive oil
salt and pepper

1. Juice both lemons, remove seeds
2. Add oil, and salt and pepper

Leftover Turkey Tetrazzini

From Shari's kitchen

1 (16-0z.) package spaghetti
½ cup margarine, melted
½ lb. fresh mushrooms, sliced
2 (10-½ oz.) cans cream of chicken soup
1 cup water
4 cups leftover turkey, sliced or cubed
1 cup shredded sharp Cheddar cheese
1 (10-oz.) pkg. frozen peas
2 tablespoons Worcestershire sauce
1 teaspoon salt
¼ teaspoon pepper
1 cup grated Parmesan cheese
Paprika

Break spaghetti into halves, prepare as package directed, drain. In large pan, sauté' mushrooms in melted margarine until tender. Stir in soup and water. Cook and stir until blended. Stir in spaghetti and all other ingredients except Parmesan cheese and paprika.

Pour into a casserole dish, top with Parmesan cheese and sprinkle with paprika. Bake at 375 for 45 minutes.

This is great with chicken as well.

Sausage Balls

From the kitchen of our late aunt, Mattie Mae Swain
Childersburg, AL

1 cup Bisquick

1 cup sharp grated cheese

1 lb. sausage

Water for consistency

Mix all ingredients, roll into balls and bake at 350 degrees until done.

Rosemary Lamb Kebabs

From Shari's kitchen

1 tablespoon ground pepper
2 teaspoons minced shallots
2 teaspoons minced fresh rosemary
1 large minced clove garlic
2 tablespoons bourbon or beef broth
1½ pounds well-trimmed lamp in 1" cubes

In a medium bowl, combine black pepper, shallots, rosemary, garlic and bourbon or broth. Add lamb an coat all sides; discard excess coating mixture. Divide and thread cubes on 6 skewers. Grill over medium for 6 to 8 minutes or until desired it's cooked as desired.

Mother's Savory Beef Stew

From the kitchen of Willie B. Quinn, Shari's mom

1 lb. cut up chuck beef
2 beef bouillon cubes
Celery
2/5 Heinz Chili Sauce
¼ ketchup
Onions
Carrots
Potatoes

Add as much water as you think. Bring to a boil and then simmer about 4 hours, adding 2/5 bottle of Heinz Chili sauce and ¼ ketchup. About ¾ an hour before ready to serve, add cut up onion, carrots and potatoes. Don't overcook vegetables.

Season to taste.

Malik's Favorite Chicken Alfredo

From Shari's kitchen

1 box of Fettuccine pasta
1 lb. of chicken breast, sliced

Alfredo Sauce:

1 stick butter
1 clove garlic, minced or freshly pressed
1 pint of heavy cream
2 tablespoons cream cheese
1 cup of freshly grated parmesan cheese
salt and pepper to taste

1. Boil pasta with olive oil until al dente per packaging.
2. Brown chicken on both sides in skillet with olive oil over medium heat. Sprinkle salt, pepper and garlic on chicken. You can also add fresh garlic to the oil in pan.
3. In a sauce pan over medium heat, melt butter and add garlic, cook for 2 minutes. Add cream and cream cheese, and heat until bubbling (not boiling).
4. Add in parmesan cheese and mix until the cheese melts. Add salt and pepper. Serve over pasta with garlic bread. Optional: Add broccoli

Honey Mustard Chicken

From Ann's kitchen

½ cup Miracle Whip Dressing (or Mayo)

2 tablespoons Dijon mustard

1 tablespoon honey

4 boneless chicken breasts (1-1¼ lbs.)

1. Heat broiler
2. Mix dressing or mayo, mustard and honey.
3. Broil chicken on broiler pan rack, 5-7 inches from heat.
4. Broil 8-10 minutes on each side or until tender, turning and brushing with honey mustard mixture during the last 3 minutes of cooking time.

Lemon Dijon Baked Fish

From Ann's kitchen

1 ½ lbs. orange roughy fillet
3 tablespoons butter, melted
1 tsp. Worcestershire sauce
⅔ cup butter flavored crackers, crushed
2 tablespoons Dijon mustard
1 tablespoon lemon juice

1. Preheat oven to 425 degrees.
2. Cut fillets in half; arrange in greased 9x13-inch baking dish.
3. Combine mustard, butter, lemon juice and Worcestershire sauce.
4. Baste mixture over fillets.
5. Place cracker in plastic bag; crush crackers with roller. Sprinkle over fillets.
6. Bake 20-25 minutes or until fish flakes easily with fork.

Beef Tips

From Ann's kitchen

2 lbs. beef tips

1 clove garlic

1 small onion, chopped

1 tablespoon margarine or olive oil

2 cans golden mushroom soup

¾ cup red cooking wine

1 small jar sliced mushrooms

1. Brown beef tips in tablespoon of margarine or olive oil with chopped onion.
2. Combine beef tips and onion in crockpot with remaining ingredients and cook on low 8-10 hours.

Serve over rice.

Jack Mack

From the kitchen of McKinley "Kenny" Johnson, Ann's brother
Albany, NY

4-6 cans Mackerel (washed and cleaned like tuna)
3-4 packages Sazón Goya
Salt & Pepper
1 large onion
1 large green pepper

Season Mackerel with Sazón, salt, pepper; sauté onion and pepper in olive oil or butter; add Mackerel and cook on low heat for 15-20 minutes.

Serve with rice and beans

Chicken and Cheese Enchiladas

From Ann's kitchen

1 medium onion
1 ½ cups shredded cooked chicken
1 3-oz pkg cream cheese, cubed
2 cups shredded extra sharp cheddar cheese
1 12-oz jar picante sauce, divided
2 tablespoons margarine
1 tsp ground cumin
8 6-inch flour tortillas

1. Heat oven to 350 degrees. Cook and stir onion in margarine in large skillet until tender.
2. Stick in chicken, ¼ picante sauce, cream cheese and cumin. Cook until thoroughly heated.
3. Stir in 1 cup cheese; spoon about ⅓ cup chicken mixture in center of each tortilla. Roll up and place seam side down in 12x7-inch baking dish.
4. Top with remaining picante sauce and cheese. Bake 15 minutes.

Easy Meatloaf

From Ann's kitchen

2 lbs. lean ground beef or turkey

1 pkg. (6-¼ oz. Stove Top Stuffing Mix for Beef)

1 cup water

½ ketchup, divided

2 eggs, beaten

Mix all ingredients except ¼ ketchup of the catsup. Shape meat mixture into oval loaf in 12x8-inch baking dish; top with remaining ¼ ketchup. Bake at 375 degrees for 1 hour or until center is no longer pink. Makes 6-8 servings.

Southern Pork Chop Casserole

From Ann's kitchen

2 tablespoons Crisco or vegetable oil

6-8 pork chops

1 cup uncooked rice

1 package of dry onion soup mix

1 can (10 ¼ ounce) mushroom soup

1. Pre-heat oven to 375 degrees.
2. Heat Crisco or vegetable oil in large skillet on medium heat. Brown pork chops.
3. Sprinkle uncooked rice in bottom or large casserole or baking dish. Sprinkle dry soup mix over rice and place pork chops on top. Pour mushroom soup over pork chops. Cover with water.
4. Bake uncovered for 1 hour.

Mustard Chicken

From Ann's kitchen

4 skinless chicken breasts

1 tablespoon minced garlic or garlic powder

salt and pepper

½ cup margarine

¼ cup yellow mustard

1. Preheat oven at 375 degrees.
2. Place chicken in greased baking dish.
3. Microwave margarine mixed with mustard and garlic until melted.
4. Stir in garlic. Pour over chicken; sprinkle with salt and pepper to taste.
5. Bake for 1 hour to 1 hour and 15 minutes.
6.

Stuffed Bell Peppers

From the kitchen of our Aunt Marie
Durham, NC

4 large bell peppers
1 lb. ground Italian sweet sausage
½ cup chopped onion
1 cup cooked rice
1 tablespoon garlic powder
2 tsp. sugar
1 tsp. black pepper
1 cup diced tomatoes
1 28oz can of tomato sauce

In a skillet, cook Italian sausage until brown and drain.

Mix ingredients together except tomato sauce, cup top of peppers or slice in half; stuff each pepper with sausage mixture. Place in baking dish, pour 28 oz. can of tomato sauce over peppers and sprinkle with parmesan cheese or shredded cheese. Cover dish with aluminum foil.

Bake for 1 hour and 15 minutes at 350.

Drunken Chicken

From Shari's kitchen

1 whole chicken
1 can of beer
Seasoning rub (your own mixture)

Season a whole chicken as you would before baking, rubbing your favorite seasoning on the chicken. Open a can of beer, stand the beer can on an oven safe plate or pan on the grill. Place the chicken over the beer can, inserting the can into the cavity of the chicken.

Close grill lid and cook the chicken for 1 to 1 ½ hours. Remove chicken from the grill and discard the beer. The flavor from the beer amazingly provides a delicious flavor for the chicken.

Side Dishes

Kitchens are made to bring families together

-*Unknown*

Ann's Macaroni & Cheese

(very large pan)
2 boxes (16 oz.) of elbow macaroni
12 eggs
3 sticks of margarine
3 cans of evaporated
32 oz. Medium cheese
16 oz. Sharp cheese
16 oz. Extra Sharp cheese
Accent, salt, pepper to season
a pinch of sugar

(large pan)
1-16 oz. box elbow macaroni
6 eggs
1 ½ sticks of margarine
1 ½ can of evaporated milk
8 oz. Medium cheese
8 oz. Sharp cheddar cheese
8 oz. Extra sharp cheese
Season with Accent, Salt and pepper
a pinch of sugar

Continued on next page

1. Cook and drain pasta as directed until al dente
2. Shred cheese,
3. In sauce pan, pour milk, melt cheese, stir constantly, add butter.
4. Pour cheese sauce
5. Beat eggs and add to mixture to macaroni and cheese mixture, season, bake
6. Cover with foil for 20 minutes, then uncover and bake at 350 degrees for approximately 30 minutes until golden brown

Optional: Add shredded cheese to the top the last 5 minutes.

Baked Macaroni & Cheese with Red Peppers

From Shari's kitchen

16 oz. mini penne pasta or elbows (I like to use penne)
2 teaspoons olive oil (add to boiling pasta water)
1 stick butter, soften and slicked
1 teaspoon yellow mustard or dry mustard
2 cans evaporated milk
2 eggs, beaten
¼ paprika
sea salt and pepper to taste
Mrs. Dash Table Blend (or low-sodium seasoning salt)
8 oz. extra sharp cheese or aged cheese
8 oz. Vermont cheddar cheese
5 oz. pepper jack cheese with jalapeños
5 oz. Monterey jack cheese
2-3 oz. Velveeta cheese
½ red pepper, finely diced

1. Cook pasta until al dente. Follow packing instructions.
2. While pasta is cooking cut cheese into cubes.
3. Drain pasta when done.
4. Put pasta in large mixing bowl, stir in all ingredients. Mix well.

Continued on next page

5. Sauté diced red peppers in small pan skillet with 2-3 tablespoons of margarine or butter. (About 3 minutes). Pour red peppers and seasoned butter into macaroni and cheese mixture. Mix well so red peppers are throughout mixture.
6. Grease casserole dish with pan spray; pour mixture into dish.
7. Bake at 350 degrees for 45 minutes; ½ way through cooking, stir mixture.
8. 10 minutes before complete, sprinkle with either shredded cheese or bread crumbs.

Other great toppings: Ritz Crackers, Homemade Biscuit Crumbs or Crumbled Cornbread.

Broccoli Cheese Casserole

From Shari's kitchen

Frozen broccoli
Minute Maid Rice
Can of Mushroom Soup
Jar of Cheez Whiz
1 stick of butter
1 cup of hot water

Preheat oven at 350 degrees

Mix frozen broccoli, rice, mushroom soup, stick of butter and a cup of hot water. Stir all ingredients together with seasoning, pour into greased baking dish and bake for 40 minutes or until brown on top.

Southern Fried Corn

From Ann's kitchen

6 ears corn
¼ cup bacon drippings or vegetable oil
2 tablespoons all-purpose flour
1 tablespoon sugar
1 cup water
¼ cup milk
Salt and pepper to taste

Shuck corn. Wash and remove silk. After cutting the kernels in half with a sharp knife, cut kernels completely off the cob. (This is called cream style cutting.) Scrape juice out of corn cob into the corn. Heat bacon drippings in a large heavy skillet. Add corn, flour, sugar, water, milk, and salt and pepper. Bring mixture to boil, stirring constantly. Cover; reduce heat and simmer, stirring occasionally, until corn is tender, about 20 to 25 minutes. If necessary, add a little hot water.

Creamy Corn Casserole *(Corn Pudding)*

From the kitchen of our Aunt Katie, Albany, NY

1 bag of frozen corn, thawed
1 can whole corn, drain liquid
1 can cream corn
½ small green pepper chopped
½ small red pepper chopped
1 medium onion
1 teaspoon salt
1 teaspoon black pepper
1 cup of sugar
1 stick of butter
4 large eggs, beat well
2 cups of milk
2 tablespoons of flour
1 tablespoon of mustard
¼ teaspoon nutmeg
½ cup to 1 cup shredded cheese

Sprinkle paprika on top and bake 350 degrees for 45 minutes or until golden brown (generally an hour).

Easy Corn Casserole II

From Shari's kitchen

1- 15 oz. can whole kernel corn, drained
1-15 oz. can cream style corn
1 package Jiffy corn muffin mix (8oz)
1 cup sour cream
½ cup butter, melted
1 cup shredded cheddar cheese or your favorite cheese

Preheat oven to 350 degrees. Mix all ingredients, except the cheese, together and pour in a greased baking dish. After the casserole has baked 45 minutes, or is set in the middle and is golden brown, sprinkle with cheese and put back in the oven. Let cheese melt, take the casserole out and enjoy this ridiculously buttery dish.

Gaye Nell's Cornbread Dressing

From the kitchen of our beloved late cousin Gaye Nell Black
Childersburg, AL

1 skillet cornbread
2 cans French onion soup
2 cans cream of celery soup
1 can chicken broth
pan dripping
salt, pepper
2 eggs
Poultry seasons

1. Mix all ingredients together
2. Bake at 350 degrees 40 minutes or until done.

Collard Greens

From Shari's kitchen

My mom and aunts make the most amazing collard greens which I have not been able to duplicate but this is delicious also.

1-2 bunches of fresh collard greens
2 pieces of smoked turkey wings
1 large sweet onion (thick slices since they'll cook down)
2 chicken bouillon cubes
1 ½ to 2 cups chicken broth
2 caps full of apple cider vinegar
2 caps full of Frank's Red Hot Sauce
2 caps full of Worcestershire Sauce
1/8 cup of sugar (optional but recommended)

Seasonings to taste: sea salt, pepper, garlic, Mrs. Dash Original Blend and red pepper flakes

I love to get my greens freshly picked from the local farmer's market. Wash and thoroughly clean greens; roll leaves and evenly slice in 1/2 inch sizes.

In a large pot, coat the bottom with olive oil, sauté sliced onions but do not brown or caramelize; pour in chicken broth, add smoked turkey, bouillon cubes and enough water to cover the turkey wings; bring to a boil then reduce to medium heat and cook for 1 hour.

Then add sliced greens and remaining ingredients; bring to a boil then reduce heat and simmer for 1 to 1 ½ hours. If needed, add additional broth or water, or discard some. I like my greens with a slight crunch so I pour out some of the broth leaving just enough to slightly cover the greens.

Sweet Potato Casserole

From Shari's kitchen

4 ½ to 5 pounds fresh sweet potatoes
4 tablespoons (1/2 stick) butter
2 large eggs, lightly beaten
1 teaspoon salt
1 teaspoon ground cinnamon
½ teaspoon vanilla extract
½ teaspoon ground nutmeg
½ cup dark brown sugar
¼ cup heavy cream

Oatmeal Cookie Crumble:
½ cup all-purpose flour
1 cup dark brown sugar
¼ teaspoon salt
1 cup quick-cooking oats
1/2 teaspoon ground cinnamon
¼ pound (1 stick) butter, at room temperature
2 cups miniature marshmallows

Preheat the oven to 350. Boil sweet potatoes until you can easily pierce with fork. Drain water. Place the cooked potatoes into a large bowl.

Mash the sweet potatoes with the butter using a potato masher until mostly smooth. Add the eggs, salt, cinnamon, vanilla, and nutmeg and beat until you have a uniform mixture. Add the brown sugar and cream and mix well. Add oatmeal cookie crust on top.

Oatmeal Cookie Crust for Sweet Potato Casserole

Combine the flour, brown sugar, salt, oats, and cinnamon in a medium bowl and stir together well. Stir in the butter with a fork until you have a crumbly mixture.

If you had turned off the oven, heat it again to 350 degrees F. Lightly coat a 9 x 13-inch baking pan with cooking spray. Spreading the sweet potatoes in the pan. Top with the marshmallows, then crumble the oatmeal crust on top of the marshmallows. Bake 30 to 45 minute

Onion Roasted Potatoes

From Ann's kitchen

1 envelope Onion or Onion-Mushroom Soup Mix
2 pounds all-purpose potatoes cut into large chunks
⅓ cup olive or vegetable oil

Preheat oven to 450. In large plastic bag or bowl, add all ingredients. Close bag and shake, or toss in bowl, until potatoes are evenly coated.

Empty potatoes into shallow or roasting pan; discard bag. Bake, stirring occasionally, for 40 minutes or until potatoes are tender and golden brown.

Makes 8 servings.

Lobster Mashed Potatoes

From Shari's kitchen

5 lbs. potatoes
1 stick of salted butter
1½-2 cups milk
2 lbs. of cooked frozen or fresh lobster
Salt and garlic to taste

Peel and boil potatoes until fork goes through them. Drain water when done.

While potatoes are boiling, sauté the cooked lobster in a sauté pan with ½ butter. Don't overcook since they are already precooked.

Melt ½ stick of butter with 1 ½ to 2 cups of milk in saucepan. Add butter mixture into potatoes, stir until creamy or the consistency you like (I like my potatoes a little lumpy). Add salt and garlic.

Add sautéed lobster to the mashed potatoes and enjoy!

Baked Cinnamon Apples

From Shari's kitchen

3 apples - peeled, cored and sliced
¾ cup water
1 tablespoon all-purpose flour
1 tablespoon cornstarch
1 tablespoon unsalted butter
½ cup packed light brown sugar
1 teaspoon ground cinnamon
¼ teaspoon sea salt

Preheat oven to 350

Arrange apple slices in 8x8 baking dish; whisk together water, flour and cornstarch, stir in butter, brown sugar, cinnamon and salt. Stir until mixture is smooth.

Pour mixture over the apples, cover dish with foil. Bake for 40 minutes until apples are tender. Stir every 10 to 15 minutes.

Can be served as breakfast item as well.

Candied Cinnamon Pecans

From Shari's kitchen

Great on Salads

½ cup pecan halves, chopped
1 tablespoon unsalted butter, melted
1 tablespoon dark brown sugar
1 teaspoon ground cinnamon

Preheat oven to 375 degrees. Line cookie sheet with parchment paper. Toss pecans in a bowl with melted butter.

Combine brown sugar and cinnamon, and toss with buttered pecans. Arrange coated pecans on wax paper-lined cookie sheet. Bake in oven for 6-8 minutes, until sugar is caramelized.

Remove cookie sheet from oven and allow to cool on parchment paper. Great over salads or ice cream, or simply enjoy.

Once cooled, store in airtight container at room temperature.

Desserts

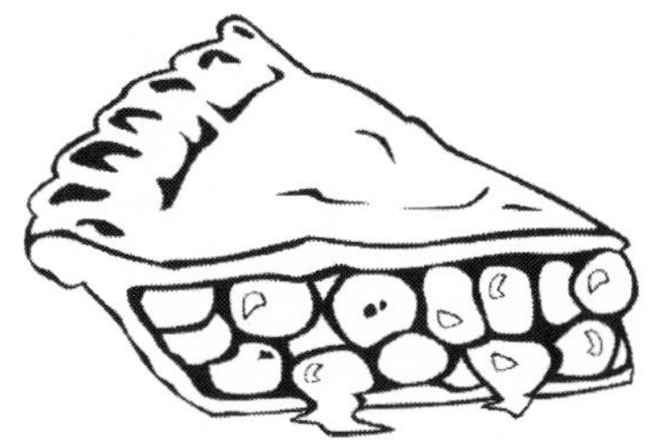

Dessert is like a feel-good song and
the best ones make you dance.
- *chef Edward Lee*

Alabama Homemade Vanilla Ice Cream

From Ann's kitchen

Both Shari and Ann's mother's used to always make homemade vanilla ice cream.

Growing up in Alabama , we used to go down to the country to our Aunt Precious' home to make this and churn it the old-fashioned way using rock salt. This is a family favorite. This recipe is very easy to make with the taste of the country. Enjoy!

2 eggs

1 ½ cups sugar

2 ½ cup milk (I use cans of evaporated milk)

2 ¼ tsp. vanilla

¼ tsp. salt (must use as salt helps it freeze and form ice crystals)

Beat eggs and gradually add sugar. Continue to beat until mixture is very stiff. Add remaining ingredients and mix thoroughly. Freeze in an ice cream maker according to manufacturer's instructions; or freeze overnight in a plastic container with lid.

Variation: add chocolate chips or mint flavoring

Pecan Pie

From the kitchen of our beloved late cousin, Pearlie Mae Hamilton Bardwell of Childersburg, AL, whom is named after our late grandmother, Pearl.

2 eggs
½ sugar
1 teaspoon vanilla
3 tablespoons butter or margarine
1 cup Karo syrup
1 cup pecans, chopped
½ teaspoon salt
1 pie shell

Beat eggs slightly; add sugar, syrup, nuts, salt and vanilla. Add chopped up butter or margarine.

Put into unbaked pie shell and bake 50 minutes at 325 degrees. The pecans will float and form crust on top if baked slowly.

Delicious Pound Cake

From Shari's kitchen

3 cups all-purpose flour, sifted
5 large eggs
3 cups sugar
1 cup softened butter
¼ teaspoon salt
½ cup vegetable shortening
1 ½ teaspoons pure vanilla extract
½ teaspoon lemon extract
1 cup lemon-lime soda

1. Preheat oven to 325 degrees, Combine flour and salt, combine remaining ingredients except soda in large bowl, beat at medium speed until light and fluffy (about 5 minutes).
2. Reduce speed to low, adding ingredients and soda (beginning and ending with dry ingredients).
3. Pour into Bundt or tube pan
4. Bake 1 ½ hours or until toothpick is clean, cool in pan for 15 minutes

Great served with warm fresh strawberries and ice cream

Mother's Southern Sweet Potato Pie

From the kitchen of Willie B. Quinn, Shari's mother

1 ½ cups cooked sweet potatoes
¾ cup sugar (½ brown; ½ white)
1 cup evaporated milk
3 cups eggs, beaten
¼ cup butter, soft
½ teaspoon salt
½ teaspoon cinnamon
½ teaspoon nutmeg
1 9-inch pie shell

Preheat oven to 450 degrees

1. Bake pie shell for 5 minutes
2. Mix all ingredients using electric mixer. Pour mixture into pie crust.
3. Bake 10 minutes, then reduce heat to 325 degrees and bake 30 minutes or until pie tests done.

Sweet Potato Pie II

From the kitchen of Ms. Minnie Comithier, Albany, NY via Greensboro, Georgia

2½ pounds sweet potatoes
¼ stick butter
¾ cup sugar
½ tsp. nutmeg
1/8 tsp. cinnamon
½ vanilla extract
1 egg
1/8 tsp karo syrup
1 deep dish pie crust

Boil potatoes until tender, drain (Ms. Minnie drains them for a couple of hours); mash with potato masher. Beat all ingredients together until smooth. Bake for 45 minutes on 350.

Great with Oronoque deep dish pie crust

Classic Banana Pudding

From Shari's kitchen

My mom always made Banana Pudding - it's a favorite and I would love to enjoy it fresh out the oven; and of course, I would eat the vanilla wafers as she prepared this.

¾ cup plus 1 tablespoon sugar
1/3 cup cornstarch
Pinch of salt
3 cups milk
8 eggs, separated
3 tablespoons butter
1 tablespoon vanilla extract
3 cups vanilla cookie wafers
4 ripe bananas, thinly sliced
½ teaspoon cream of tartar

Preheat oven to 350.

Combine ½ cup sugar, cornstarch and salt in a large saucepan; stir until blended. Stir in milk. Cook over medium heat, stirring constantly until thickened and boiling; boil 1 minute, then remove from heat.

In small bowl whisk egg yolks, then whisk in about ½ cup of the hot custard until blended. Pour yolk mixture back into custard in saucepan; cook over medium heat, stirring, for 2 minutes. Stir in butter and vanilla until blended.

Place half the vanilla wafers on bottom of 2-quart casserole. Top with layers of banana slices and custard. Repeat layers, ending with custard.

Beat egg whites and ¼ cup sugar in large mixing bowl at low speed until frothy. Add cream of tartar, increase speed to medium and gradually beat in remaining sugar. Beat until whites just hold stiff peaks.

Spoon meringue over hot custard, evenly spreading to the edges of the casserole dish. Bake in oven for 20 minutes or until golden brown.

Remove from oven and cool - and enjoy!

Blackberry Dumpling

From the kitchen of our Aunt Marie, Durham, NC

Dumpling:
2 cups all-purpose flour
1 tsp. salt
¾ cup Crisco shortening
2 tsp. butter, cold
6 tsp. ice water

Sift together flour and salt, and cut in Crisco. Mix ingredients until crumbly. Add ice water. Roll dough about ¼ -inch thick. Cut out dough with biscuit cutter. Follow steps below to make berry mixture.

Berry Filling:
(4) 6 oz. packages of fresh blackberries
4 cups cold water
2 ½ cups sugar
2 tsp. vanilla
½ tsp. nutmeg
2 tsp. flour

1. Mix ingredient in a Dutch oven. Bring to a boil and simmer for 10 minutes. Place 1-2 tablespoons of berries in center of crust and pinch edges together.
2. Bring remaining berries and juice to a boil; mix 2 teaspoons of flour with water, and pour into the berries juice.
3. Place berry-filled dumpling pieces in one at a time into the Dutch oven.
4. Place Dutch oven in oven at 350. Cook uncovered for ½ hour.

Serves 8 - Top with ice cream and whipping topping

Peanut Butter Balls

This recipe was shared with me from a co-worker who made these for a holiday office party. They are incredible.

1 stick of butter or margarine
1 lb. of confectioners' sugar (1 box or half a bag)
2 cups of peanut butter
3 cups of Rice Krispie cereal

1. Mix all ingredients in a large bowl and roll into tablespoon size balls, place on a cookie sheet and put in refrigerator to firm balls for 30 minutes.
2. Melt almond bark in double boiler, using a separate plastic bowl roll balls in chocolate to coat, place them back on cookie sheet and return to refrigerator to harden chocolate.

No Bake Cheesecake

From Shari's kitchen

8 oz. softened cream cheese
⅓ cup sugar
8 oz. cool whip
2 tablespoons lemon juice
Graham Cracker pie crust

1. Cream sugar and cream cheese, fold in with cool whip with spatula or spoon, add lemon juice, mix well.
2. Pour into pie crust, place in refrigerator for 2 hours to chill; add desired fruit toppings.

La Strawberry Romanoff

From Shari's kitchen

½ cup sour cream
¼ cup packed brown sugar
2 tablespoons brandy
½ cup heavy cream
¼ cup powdered sugar
2 pints strawberries, hulled

Whisk together the sour cream and brown sugar. Stir until the sugar is blended well; stir in brandy; whip heavy cream until soft peak forms. Add powdered sugar and whip until cream forms stiff peaks.

Fold the whipped cream into the sour cream mixture until the mixtures are well blended.

Serve over fresh strawberries

Lemon Sunshine Cake

From Shari's kitchen

1 cup butter, soft
2 cups sugar
4 eggs
2 ¾ cup flour
¼ teaspoon baking soda
1 cup sour cream
1 teaspoon orange juice
2 teaspoons lemon extract
1 teaspoon vanilla extract

1. Preheat oven to 325 degrees
2. Beat butter and sugar until creamy; add eggs, one at a time, beating after each
3. In another bowl, mix flour and baking soda; add to butter mixture alternately with sour cream.
4. Stir in remaining ingredients. Spoon batter into greased Bundt or tube pan.
5. Bake 60-65 minutes or until inserted toothpick is clean.

Best Damn Lemon Cake Ever

From the kitchen of Ms. Willie B. Quinn, Shari's mother

½ cup blanched almonds (finely grind in food processor)

1 ½ cups sifted all-purpose flour

1 teaspoon baking powder

¾ teaspoon salt

1 stick of butter, softened

1 cup sugar

2 eggs

½ cup milk

1 1-ounce bottle of lemon extract

Finely grated rind of 2 extra-large or 3 medium size lemons (reserve juice for glaze)

1. Adjust oven rack ⅓ up from bottom of the oven; preheat oven at 350 degrees.
2. Grease loaf pan and sprinkle flour.
3. In a small sauce pan melt butter on low heat.
4. Pour butter in large mixing bowl; add sugar and mix with electric mixer.
5. On low speed, beat in the eggs one at a time, beating only to mix well.

6. Add sifted dry ingredients in 3 additions alternating with milk in 2 additions, scraping the bowl with a rubber spatula and beating until mixed after each addition. Mix in the lemon extract.
7. Stir in grated lemon grind and the ground almonds. Pour into greased pan.
8. Bake for 65 to 70 minutes or until inserted toothpick is clean.
9. Prepare glaze 3-5 minutes before cake is done.
10. Remove cake when done, let it stand 2-3 minutes, then brush hot glaze over the hot cake; the glaze should take 5 minutes to apply it all.
11. Gently invert the cake onto cooling rack.
12. When cake is completely cool, wrap in plastic wrap or aluminum foil and let stand 12-14 hours before serving; or place in the freezer for 2 hours.

Lemon glaze:

⅓ cup plus 2 tablespoons sugar

⅓ cup fresh lemon juice

Stir sugar and juice in a small saucepan over moderate heat only until sugar is dissolved; do not boil.

Willie B.'s Tea Cakes

From the kitchen of Ms. Willie B. Quinn, Shari's mother
Similar to Sugar Cookies - Delicious!

3 ½ cups sifted flour
2 ½ teaspoon baking powder
½ teaspoon salt
⅔ cup butter or margarine
1 ½ cup sugar
1 ½ teaspoon vanilla
2 eggs
1 tablespoon milk

1. Mix dry ingredients together
2. Cream butter, gradually add sugar until light and fluffy
3. Add vanilla and eggs, one at a time, beat after each egg
4. Mix together gradually
5. Wrap in foil or plastic, chill in refrigerator for several hours or overnight.
6. Preheat oven to 400 degrees
7. Roll on lightly flour surface; slice off or use cookie cutter
8. Sprinkle with sugar.
9. Bake at 400 degrees on ungreased cookie or use wax paper, bake for 8-9 minutes or until edges or lightly brown.

Shari's thebomb.com Chocolate Chip Cookies

2 ½ cups all-purpose flour
1 tsp baking soda
1 teaspoon salt
¾ cup margarine, softened
¾ cup firmly packed brown sugar
¾ cup granulated sugar
1 egg
1 tsp. vanilla extract
1 tsp. almond extract (or just 2 tsp. vanilla)
1 cup semi-sweet chocolate chips

Preheat oven to 350. Combine flour, baking soda and salt. Set aside

In a large bowl, cream together butter, brown sugar and granulated sugar together until creamy; add flour mixture until well combined.

Fold in chocolate chips. Use a cookie scooper to make uniform cookies. Line cookie sheet with wax paper and very light spray.

Placed scooped dough on wax paper. Bake 7 minutes (after 3.5 minutes turn cookie sheet around in oven to evenly cook).

Cool on wire rack and enjoy!

Chewy Oatmeal Raisin Cookies

From Shari's kitchen

2 sticks margarine softened
1 cup firmly packed brown sugar
½ cup granulated sugar
2 eggs
1 teaspoon vanilla
1 ½ cups all-purpose flour
1 teaspoon baking soda
1 teaspoon cinnamon
½ teaspoon salt
3 cups oats, uncooked
1 cup raisins

Heat oven to 350 degrees. Beat together margarine and sugars until creamy. Add eggs and vanilla; beat well. Add combined flour, baking soda, cinnamon and salt, mix well. Stir in oats and raisins; mix well.

Line cookie sheet with wax paper and lightly spray with pan spray. Drop by rounded tablespoons onto wax paper. I use small cookie scooper. Bake 8-9 minutes (I turn the tray around in over half way through baking for even baking).

Cool on wire rack.

Lemon Meringue Pie

From the kitchen of Nina F. Marbury, Ann's sister
Childersburg, AL

1 can sweetened condensed milk

2 egg yolks - Save the whites to make meringue

½ cup Lemon Juice

1 Graham Cracker pie shell

Mix together really well and pour into pie shell

Meringue

2 egg whites

¼ cup sugar

1 Tablespoon cream of tartar

Beat egg whites well. Add sugar and mix well at high speed. Gradually add cream of tartar, beat well until it makes a peak. Spread over pie and bake in preheated over at 350 degrees until brown. Watch carefully to avoid over baking.

Easy Fruity Cake

From the kitchen of our cousin, Lovie Jean Barnes, whom is named after our late great-grandmother Mama Lovie

1 box cake mix
¼ cup oil
1 can pie filling - any flavor
½ cup water
1 eggs

Pour oil in 13x9x2 inch pan. Place other ingredients in pan and stir well until blended. Pour in pie filling and stir with fork for marble affect. Bake at 350 degree for 40-50 minutes.

Lemon Meringue Pie II

From Shari's kitchen

Pastry

1 cup Gold Medal™ all-purpose flour
½ teaspoon salt
1/3 cup plus 1 tablespoon shortening
2-3 tablespoons cold water

Filling

3 egg yolks
1 ½ cups sugar
1/3 cup plus 1 tablespoon cornstarch
1 ½ cups water
3 tablespoons butter or margarine
2 teaspoons grated lemon peel
½ cup lemon juice
2 drops yellow food color (optional)

Meringue

3 egg whites
¼ teaspoon cream of tartar
6 tablespoons sugar
½ teaspoon vanilla

In medium bowl, mix flour and salt. Cut in shortening, using pastry blender (or pulling 2 table knives through ingredients in opposite directions), until particles are size of small peas. Sprinkle with cold water, 1 tablespoon at a time, tossing with fork until all flour is moistened and pastry almost cleans side of bowl (1 to 2 teaspoons more water can be added if necessary).

Gather pastry into a ball. Shape into flattened round on lightly floured surface. Wrap in plastic wrap; refrigerate about 45 minutes or until dough is firm and cold, yet pliable. This allows the shortening to become slightly firm, which helps make the baked pastry more flaky. If refrigerated longer, let pastry soften slightly before rolling.

Heat oven to 475°F. With floured rolling pin, roll pastry into round 2 inches larger than upside-down 9-inch glass pie plate. Fold pastry into fourths; place in pie plate. Unfold and ease into plate, pressing firmly against bottom and side. Trim overhanging edge of pastry 1 inch from rim of pie plate. Fold and roll pastry under, even with plate; flute as desired. Prick bottom and side of pastry thoroughly with fork. Bake 8 to 10 minutes or until light brown; cool on cooling rack.

Reduce oven temperature to 400°F. In small bowl, beat egg yolks with fork. In 2-quart saucepan, mix sugar and cornstarch; gradually stir in water. Cook over medium heat, stirring constantly, until mixture thickens and boils. Boil and stir 1 minute.

Immediately stir at least half of hot mixture into egg yolks; stir back into hot mixture in saucepan. Boil and stir 2 minutes; remove from heat. Stir in butter, lemon peel, lemon juice and food color. Pour into pie crust.

In medium bowl, beat egg whites and cream of tartar with electric mixer on high speed until foamy. Beat in sugar, 1 tablespoon at a time; continue beating until stiff and glossy. Do not under beat. Beat in vanilla. Spoon onto hot pie filling. Spread over filling, carefully sealing meringue to edge of crust to prevent shrinking or weeping.

Bake 8 to 12 minutes or until meringue is light brown. Cool away from draft 2 hours. Cover and refrigerate cooled pie until serving. Store in refrigerator.

Coconut Pie

From the kitchen of Ms. Minnie Comithier, Albany, NY via Greensboro, Georgia

Makes 3 pies:

4 large eggs
½ pound of butter
3 cups granulated sugar
½ cup flour
1 can of carnation milk
1 quart of milk
1 teaspoon vanilla extract
8 oz. bag of coconut
3 deep dish pie crusts

In a large bowl cream eggs, sugar and butter until smooth. Add milk, flour and vanilla flavoring. You can add coconut in this mixture or you can add coconut after you pour the liquid mixture into your pre-made pie crusts.

Bake 45-50 minutes at 350.

To make one (1) pie: Divide the ingredients by a third. However, add half a teaspoon of vanilla.

Fluffy Cotton Cake

From Shari's kitchen

1 Box Duncan Hines Golden Butter cake mix
½ cup Crisco
4 eggs at room temperature
1 (11 oz.) can of Mandarin oranges (retain juice)

Mix all ingredients with an electric mixer including Mandarin juice, divide mixture into 3 round 9-inch pans that have been greased and floured.

Bake at 325 degrees for 20 minutes. Allow to completely cool.

Icing:

1 small box of instant vanilla pudding mix
1 large can crushed pineapples with juice
1 (13 oz.) container of Cool Whip

Mix above ingredients together with an electric mixer. Spread mixture between each layer, on tops and sides.

Chill in refrigerator before serving. Can be made one (1) day in advance.

Strawberry Pie

From Shari's kitchen

2 ready-made pie crust sheets
2 tablespoons butter, melted
5 cups sliced fresh strawberries, washed and hulled
½ cup granulated sugar
3 tablespoons cornstarch
Pinch of salt
Sprinkle of granulated sugar for top crust

Roll out 1 sheet of the pie crust and put in a 9-inch pie dish, pressing the edges on pie plate. Roll out the other sheet and cut into strips

In a medium bowl, mix together all of the filling ingredients and pour into the crust.

Arrange the strips over the top of the pie in a crisscross pattern, tucking or pressing the edges, Brush the top with the melted butter and sprinkle sugar.

Bake for 25 minutes and then reduce the temperature to 350 degrees and bake another 30 minutes until the top is golden brown.

Serve with ice cream or whipped cream

Congealed Salad

From the kitchen of Nina Faye Marbury, Ann's Sister
Childersburg, AL

1-6 oz. pkg. lime Jell-O
1-3 oz. pkg. lemon Jell-O
18 oz. pkg. creamed cheese
3 cups boiling water
2 tablespoons vinegar
24 large marshmallows
Medium can crushed pineapples, drained

1. Combine Jell-O and marshmallows with boiling water until dissolved.
2. Chill until consistency of egg whites.
3. Cream cheese with vinegar and pineapple.
4. Fold into Jell-O mixture. Chill until set.

Autumn Apple Crisp

From the kitchen of our cousin LaQuanda Lawson, Albany, NY

Preheat oven to 375 degrees

Filling:

½ cup confectioners' sugar
½ cup brown sugar
2 tablespoons flour
5 cups peeled and cored apples (approx. 5 apples) sliced thin

Combine all ingredients and spoon into deep pie shell

Topping:

¾ cup flour
½ cup teaspoon cinnamon
⅓ cup softened butter or oil

Combine to form crumbs and sprinkle on pie. Bake at 375 degrees for 40-45 minutes or until golden brown.

Cinnamon Apple Cake

From Shari's kitchen

⅓ cup brown sugar
1 teaspoon ground cinnamon
⅔ cup white sugar
½ cup butter, softened
2 eggs
1 ½ teaspoons vanilla extract
1 ½ cups all-purpose flour
½ cup milk
1 apple, peeled, cored and chopped

1. Preheat oven to 350 degrees, grease and flour a 9x5 inch loaf pan.
2. Mix brown sugar and cinnamon together in a bowl.
3. Beat white sugar and butter together in a bowl using an electric mixer until smooth and creamy. Beat in eggs, 1 at a time, until blended, all vanilla extract.
4. Combine flour and baking powder together in a bowl; stir into creamed butter mixture. Mix milk into batter until smooth. Pour half the batter into the prepared loaf pan; add half the apples and half the brown sugar mixture. Lightly pat apple mixture into batter. Pour remaining batter over apple layer; top with remaining apples and brown sugar mixture. Lightly pat apple into batter; swirl brown sugar mixture through apple with a fork.
5. Bake for 30 to 40 minutes or until inserted toothpick comes out clean.

No Bake Peanut Butter Pie

From Shari's kitchen

1 chocolate pie crust
1 package cream cheese
1 cup peanut butter
1 cup sugar
1 tablespoon butter
1 teaspoon vanilla
1 cup heavy whipping cream

Mix all ingredients together except whipping cream. In a separate bowl beat heavy whipping cream until thick and then fold into mixture. Pour into pie crust shell and refrigerate.

Banana Coconut Upside Down Cake

From Shari's kitchen

1 yellow cake mix
3 eggs
1/3 cup oil
1/2 cup sour cream
1/2 water
small box of instant vanilla pudding mix
6-7 bananas (sliced 1/4 in. thick)
2 cups shredded coconut
1/2 cup butter
1 cup packed brown sugar
2 T. lemon juice

Preheat oven to 350 degrees. Combine cake mix, eggs, oil, sour cream, water and instant pudding mix.

Grease (2) 8 or 9" round cake pans. Layer bottom of both pans with sliced bananas.

Continued on next page

In a saucepan, melt butter and add brown sugar and lemon juice. Stir until completely melted and combined. Pour sauce over bananas. Top each pan with 1 cup of the shredded coconut.

Divide cake batter in half and pour evenly into pans. Bake for 35-40 minutes. Let rest 5-10 minutes and invert on serving plate. Bananas may stay in the pan simply pull them out and arrange on cake.

Chocolate Merlot Cupcakes

From Shari's kitchen

I met a wonderful lady who sat at our dinner table during a Hibachi dinner with my son Malik for his birthday. She and her family were also celebrating her daughter's birthday and she shared these deliciously moist cupcakes with us, and later shared the recipe.

Duncan Hines Chocolate cake mix
1 package instant chocolate pudding
1 ½ cup red wine
3 eggs
½ cup canola oil

Prepare cake mix as directed but add the red wine in place of water. Mix in pudding mix. Fill cupcake liner ⅔ filled. Bake according to package instructions. Bake approximately 20 minutes.

Frost with either Red Wine Frosting or Buttercream Frosting.

Red Wine Frosting

From Shari's kitchen

This recipe was part of the shared recipe from the wonderful woman I met during Hibachi dinner for Malik's birthday.

1 can Duncan Hines frosting, vanilla
½ cup confectioners' sugar
6 tablespoons of red wine

Combine frosting, confectioners' sugar and red wine. Mix well. Top each cupcake with piped frosting.

Buttercream Frosting

From Shari's kitchen

½ cup vegetable shortening

½ cup (1 stick) unsalted butter

1 teaspoon vanilla

4 cups (approx.) confectioners' sugar

2 tablespoons milk

Cream shortening and butter with electric mixer. Add vanilla, then add sugar, a little at a time on medium speed. When mixed well, add milk until light and fluffy.

Makes approximately 3 cups of frosting.

Wedding Cake Frosting

From Shari's kitchen

2 ½ cups powdered sugar

½ cup milk

½ teaspoon almond

1 teaspoon vanilla

⅓ cup shortening

1. Beat all ingredients together until light and fluffy.
2. Spread over cupcakes or cake.

Cool Cake

From Shari's kitchen

½ cup margarine
¼ cup brown sugar
½ cup chopped walnuts
½ teaspoon vanilla extract
8 oz. cream cheese
1 cup confectioners' sugar
2 packages chocolate instant pudding
3 cups milk
1 container of cool whip

1. Mix together the first 4 ingredients until crumbles: margarine, brown sugar, chopped walnuts and vanilla. Pressed into lightly greased 13x9 pan. Bake at 350 degrees for 12 minutes. Cool before putting first layer on.
2. Beat cream cheese and sugar, then add 1 cup of cool whip. Spread over cooled crust.
3. Mix pudding and spread on second layer; then spread remaining cool whip on top. Set in fridge to chill.

Sweet Potato Pecan Pie with Bourbon Sauce

From Shari's kitchen

1 ¼ cup cooked, mashed sweet potatoes
¼ cup brown sugar
1/4 cup granulated sugar
1 egg, lightly beaten
¼ cup heavy whipping cream
¼ teaspoon vanilla extract
1 pinch salt
¾ teaspoon ground cinnamon
¾ teaspoon allspice
¾ teaspoon nutmeg
3 tablespoons softened butter
1 (9-10" size) unbaked pie pastry for a single crust

Pie Filling:

1 ¼ cup sugar
1 ¼ cup dark corn syrup
3 eggs, lightly beaten
3 tablespoons unsalted butter, softened
¼ teaspoon vanilla extract
1 pinch salt
¾ teaspoon ground cinnamon
1 ¼ cup chopped pecans

Continued on next page

Bourbon Sauce:
1 ½ cup heavy whipping cream
1 cup milk
1 package instant vanilla pudding mix (4-serving size)
3 tablespoons bourbon, brandy or rum
1 teaspoon vanilla extract

Preheat oven to 325 degrees. Combine mashed sweet potatoes, sugars, egg, cream, vanilla, salt, cinnamon, allspice, nutmeg and butter in an electric mixing bowl and beat at medium-low speed until smooth, do not overmix.

To assemble pie, spoon sweet potato filling into the pastry-lined pie pan. Fill shell evenly to the top with pecan filling. Bake 1½ hours or until a knife inserted into the center of the pie comes out clean. Store pie at room temperature for 24 hours.

Serve pie slices with Bourbon Sauce on top or to the side.

Prepare Pecan Pie Filling: Combine sugar, syrup, eggs, butter, vanilla, salt and cinnamon in an electric mixing bowl and beat on low speed until syrup is opaque, about 4-5 minutes. Stir in pecans, mix well.

Prepare Bourbon Sauce: Combine cream and milk in a large mixing bowl. Slowly whip in pudding mix. Add bourbon and continue whipping. Add vanilla and whip until mixture is well blended to sauce consistency (should not be as firm as pudding, but should not be runny). Sauce should be made about one hour before use; it will thicken as it sits.

Million Dollar Pound Cake

From Ann's kitchen

This is a favorite recipe from Ann's in-laws, the Griffin-Taylor family, that made was for Sunday dinners and all holidays.

4 cups flour
3 cups sugar
1 lb. butter
6 eggs
1 teaspoon almond flavoring
1 teaspoon vanilla flavoring
¾ cup milk

Cream butter and sugar; add eggs and flavoring mix well alternating flour with milk - mix very well. Bake at 300 degrees for 1 hour 40 minutes.

Butternut Pound Cake

From the kitchen of the late Barbara Johnson Shepard, Ann's mom

1 ½ cup Crisco
2 ¼ cups sugar
2 ½ cups plain flour
½ cup self-rising flour
1 cup milk
6 eggs
1-2 teaspoons Butter Nut and Vanilla Flavoring

Cream Crisco and sugar. Add eggs 1 at a time. Beat well. Add flour alternating with milk. Add flavoring. Bake at 325 for 1 hour.

Turn oven to 350 for 15 minutes longer or when toothpick is clear. (Secret is creaming sugar and Crisco).

Aunt Margaret's Red Velvet Cake

From the kitchen of our late Aunt Margaret McMillian, Childersburg, AL; Aunt Margaret was also Barbara Johnson Shepard's identical twin sister.

2 eggs
1 ½ cups sugar
1 ½ cup oil
1 cup buttermilk
1 teaspoon vanilla
1 teaspoon cocoa
1 oz. bottle red food color
2 cups flour, sifted
¼ teaspoon salt
1 teaspoon baking soda
1 teaspoon vinegar

Mix together in order given. Bake at 350 degrees for 30-35 minutes or until inserted toothpick is clean.

Aunt Margaret's Icing for Red Velvet Cake

From the kitchen of our late Aunt Margaret McMillian, Childersburg, AL.

1 stick butter
1 teaspoon vanilla
1 cup pecans
8 oz. cream cheese
1 box confectioner's sugar

Cream butter, cheese and sugar. Add pecan and vanilla. Spread over cool cake.

Dump Cake

From Ann's kitchen

1 Pie Filling (Your choice of cherry, Strawberry or Blueberry)

1 can pineapple (crushed)

Nuts crushed

1 Box cake mix according to the box (just wet)

Pats of butter to cover area

Bake in 9x13 pan at 325 until brown

Watergate Cake with Cover Up Frosting

From Ann's kitchen

Cake:

1 package white cake mix
1 cup oil
1 package instant pistachio pudding
3 eggs
1 cup club soda or ginger ale

Frosting:

1 package instant pistachio pudding mix
1 ¼ cups cold milk
1 container whipped topping
½ cups chopped pecans or walnuts

For the cake: Combine cake mix, oil, pudding mix and eggs and beat with a mixer for 4 minutes. Add soda and mix. Pour into a greased 9x13-inch pan. Bake at 350 degrees for 40 minutes.

For the frosting: Beat pudding mix with milk for 2 minutes. Stir in whipped topping and nuts. Spread on cake.

Liquor Cake

From Ann's kitchen

Cake:

1-18 ½ oz. Duncan Hines Yellow cake mix
1-3 ¾ oz. package Instant Vanilla Pudding Mix
1/8 cup water
4 eggs
½ cup cold water
½ cup oil
1 cup chopped pecans or walnuts
½ cup dark rum

Glaze:

⅛ lb. butter or margarine
½ cup sugar
¼ cup dark rum

Combine cake ingredients in large bowl. Beat at medium speed for 2 minutes. Pour into greased and floured 10-inch tube or 12-cup Bundt pan. Bake at 325 for 1 hour. Set on rack to cool. Invert on serving plate. Prick top immediately; drizzle and brush half of glaze evenly over top and sides. Reserve half of glaze. After cake has cooled, reheat glaze and brush it evenly over cake. Just before serving, sift 1 tablespoon powdered sugar over cake.

To make glaze: melt butter in saucepan. Stir in water and sugar. Boil 3 minutes, stirring constantly. Remove from heat and stir in Southern Comfort.

Rum Cake

From Ann's kitchen

This was first cake Ann made for the holidays after getting married

Cake:

1-18 ½ oz. yellow cake mix
1 cup chopped pecans or walnuts
1-¾ box instant vanilla pudding
4 eggs
2 cups cold water
½ cup vegetable oil
½ cup dark Bacardi rum (80 proof)

Glaze:

¼ lb. butter
¼ cup water
½ cup dark rum
1 cup sugar

Preheat oven to 325. grease and flour 10-inch tube or 12 cup Bundt pan. Sprinkle nuts over bottom of pan. Mix all cake ingredients together. Pour batter over nuts. Bake 1 hour. Cool. Invert on serving plate. Prick top of cake and drizzle glaze evenly over top and sides. Allow cake to absorb glaze. Repeat until all glaze is used.

To make glaze: melt butter in sauce pan, stir in water and sugar. Boil 5 minutes stirring constantly. Remove from heat and stir in rum. Decorate cake plate with maraschino cherries and seedless green grapes dusted with powdered sugar.

Cream Cheese Pound Cake

From Ann's kitchen

1 cup margarine, softened

½ cup butter, softened (do not substitute)

1-8 oz. package cream cheese, softened

3 cups sugar

6 eggs

3 cups cake flour, sifted

2 teaspoons vanilla extract

Combine first 3 ingredients - beat well with a heavy duty mixer. Gradually add sugar, beat until light and fluffy (about 5 minutes). Add eggs, one at a time beat well after each addition. Add flour to creamed mixture beat well. Stir in vanilla. Pour batter into a well-greased 10 inch tube pan. Bake at 325 degrees for 1 hour 30 minutes or until cake tests done. Cool in pan 10 minutes; remove from pan, and cool completely. Yield one 10-inch cake.

Strawberry Pound Cake

A favorite cake from Ann's kitchen

Ann's brother, Kenny, insists she make this for all family cookout and functions, and holidays.

1 box yellow cake mix

1 box strawberry Jell-O

4 eggs

4 tablespoon flour

1 cup vegetable oil

1-10 oz. box frozen strawberries, thawed

In large bowl mix cake mix, Jell-O and flour until mixture turns red. Add oil and eggs and mix well. Stir in strawberries with wooden spoon and mix well. Pour into greased and floured tube pan and bake at 350 for 50-60 minutes.

Five Flavor Pound Cake

From Ann's kitchen

3 cups flour, sifted
2 cups sour cream
1 teaspoon coconut flavor
1 teaspoon baking soda
4 eggs
1 teaspoon lemon flavor
1 teaspoon salt
1 teaspoon almond flavor
1 stick butter
1 teaspoon vanilla flavor
2 ½ cups sugar
1 teaspoon rum flavor

Mix dry ingredients together and set aside. Mix butter, sugar, sour cream and eggs. Alternate into dry ingredients and add flavors and mix well. Fold into prepared greased and floured Bundt pan. Bake at 325 for 1 hour or until toothpaste comes out clean.

Glaze:

1 cup powdered sugar
1 teaspoon salt
1 teaspoon vanilla
Lemon Zest enough for desired consistency.
Spoon glaze over warm cake.

Coconut Pecan Frosting

From Ann's kitchen

1 cup evaporated milk
1 cup sugar
3 slightly beaten eggs yolks
½ cup butter or margarine
1 teaspoon vanilla
1 ½ cups flaked coconut
1 cup chopped pecans

1. Combine evaporated milk, sugar, egg yolks, butter and vanilla in a saucepan.
2. Cook over medium heat, stirring until thickened about 12 minutes.
3. Remove from heat; add coconut and pecans.
4. Cool until thick enough to spread, beating occasionally.

Makes 2 ½ cups

Ann's Zebra Brownies

These were always a favorite growing up at Ann's in Rochester, NY

Filling:

2 3-oz package cream cheese, softened
¼ cup sugar
½ teaspoon vanilla
1 egg

Brownies:

22 ½ pkg. Pillsbury Deluxe Fudge Brownie Mix
½ cup very hot tap water
⅓ cup oil
1 egg

Heat oven to 350 degree. Generously grease bottom only of 13x9-inch pan. In a small bowl, blend all filling ingredients; beat at medium speed until smooth, about 1 minute. Set aside. In large bowl, combine all brownie ingredients; beat 50 strokes with a spoon. Spread half of batter in prepared pan. Pour cream cheese mixture over batter, spreading to cover. Place spoonful of remaining brownie batter on top of cream cheese. Marble by pulling knife through batter in wide curves, then turn pan and repeat.

Bake at 350 for 30-35 minutes. Cool before cutting.

Delicious Peanut Butter Cookies

From the kitchen of Willie B. Quinn, Shari's mom

My mom used to make these all the time when I was growing up. These are incredibly delicious. Your family will enjoy them! - Shari

¾ cup creamy peanut butter

½ cup (½ stick) butter flavor Crisco shortening

1-¼ cups packed light brown sugar

3 tablespoons milk

1 tablespoon vanilla

1 egg

1-¾ cups all-purpose flour

¾ teaspoon salt

¾ teaspoon baking soda

1. Preheat oven to 375 degrees.
2. Combine peanut butter, Crisco, brown sugar, milk and vanilla in large bowl.
3. Beat at medium speed until blended well. Add egg and beat just until blended.
4. Combine flour, salt and baking soda; add to creamed mixture on low speed.

Continued on next page

5. Use a small cookie scooper and drop onto ungreased cookie sheet or use wax paper. Lightly press crisscross pattern with fork.
6. Bake for 6 minutes; after 1st 3 minutes turn cookie sheet around in oven to evenly bake.
7. Cool on cooling rack or sheet of aluminum foil. Enjoy!

Sauces

The most indispensable ingredient of all good home cooking: love for those you are cooking for.

-- *Sophia Loren*

Alfredo Sauce

From Shari's kitchen

1 stick butter
1 clove garlic, minced or pressed (I use a garlic press)
1 pint of heavy cream
2 tablespoons cream cheese
1 cup of shredded parmesan cheese
salt and pepper to taste; I also sprinkle garlic powder

Fresh shredded parmesan cheese in a container from the deli or refrigerated section is best, it gives the sauce a nice rich flavor but grated or plastic-packaged will do)

1. In a sauce pan over medium heat, melt butter and add garlic, cook for 2 minutes.
2. Add cream and cream cheese, and heat until bubbling (not boiling).
3. Add in parmesan cheese and mix until the cheese melts.
4. Add salt and pepper

Serve with pasta or on top of grits and enjoy!

Tip: Add sautéed shrimp and sautéed sliced red peppers to the sauce and serve over grits - Delicious!

Shari's Crockpot Autumn Applesauce

8 apples (I like to pick fresh apples from the apple orchard: Fuji, Honeycrisp, McIntosh, Red Delicious)

1 tablespoon fresh lemon juice

¾ cup sugar (I use Stevia for sugar-free)

1 teaspoon ground cinnamon

1 teaspoon nutmeg

1 cup apple cider (or water)

1. Wash, peel, core and thinly slice apples. (Sometimes I leave the skin on for color and texture, optional).
2. Toss with lemon juice to prevent discoloration.
3. Combine apples with all ingredients and pour in slow cooker on high setting for 3 hours; or low for 6 hours.

Serve hot or cold. I love it hot! Can also store in mason jars for 3 months in refrigerator or up to a year in the freezer.

This page is intentionally left blank for my cousin

Derrius' Finger-licking Homemade BBQ Sauce

which he will not share ☺

Beverages

We don't own our family history.
We simply preserve it
for the next generation.

Rosemary Alva

Holiday Wassail Punch

From Shari's kitchen

1 quart apple juice
1 quart orange juice
2 cups cranberry juice
1 can of pineapple nectar
½ - 1 cup of sugar
3-4 cinnamon sticks
8 whole allspice berries
4 whole cloves
1 navel orange, sliced

Preparation:

Combine all ingredients in 4-quart or larger crock pot, stirring until sugar dissolves. Cook on low for 4 hours and keep warm for serving. If not using crockpot, heat mixture to a low boil for 2 minutes, then simmer for at least 1 hour before serving.

Holiday Eggnog

From Ann's kitchen - a Christmas and New Year's favorite

6 eggs
2 qt. regular milk
1 can evaporated milk
1 can sweeten condensed milk
3 /4 bottle Jamaican Rum
Sprinkle little vanilla & nutmeg
Blend all ingredients together

Rum Punch

From Ann's kitchen

This was introduced to the family at Ann's bridal show which she continues to make for gatherings and card parties

32 oz. Hawaii Punch
12 oz. frozen lemon aide
12 oz. frozen orange juice
16 oz. rum

Combine and serve.

Rum Eggnog

From Ann's kitchen

6 eggs
2/4 cups sugar
2 cups Whipped cream
1 cup cream
1 cup milk
2 cups dark rum
Groud nutmeg

Chill liquid ingredients before mixing. Separate egg whites from yolks. Beat yolks. Continue beating and add sugar. Stir in whipped cream, milk, cream and dark rum. Beat egg whites and fold in. Dust with nutmeg and chill. Makes 10 5 oz. servings.

Killer Colada
From Ann's kitchen

3 ounces coconut rum
3 tbsp. coconut milk
3 tbsp. crushed pineapples
2 cup crushed ice

Blend at high speed. Pour into chilled hurricane glass and garnish with a pineapple wedge and 2 cherries.

Coconut Passion
From Ann's kitchen

1 ounce coconut rum
5 ounces pineapple juice

Combine and serve over ice.

House Punch

From Ann's kitchen

1 cup light brown sugar, packed
4 cups water
9 lemons
2 cups pineapple juice
½ fifth dark rum
½ cognac
4 tablespoons peach brandy

Mix sugar and water in a pan and boil 5 minutes. Squeeze the juice from the lemons and pour it into the hot syrup. Add lemons rinds. Cool the syrup and refrigerate overnight. Just before serving, remove lemon rinds. Add the pineapple juice and liquors. Pack a large punch bowl with crushed ice. Pour punch over the ice and serve. Makes 10 to 15 servings.

Zombie

From Ann's kitchen

2 ounces light rum
1 ounce light rum
1 ounce lime juice
1 ounce pineapple juice
1 ounce orange juice
½ ounce apricot brandy
½ ounce 151-proof rum

Blend all ingredients except the rum. Pour into a tall Collins glass and float 151 on top. Garnish with orange twist, lime wedge, mint sprig and a cherry.

Strawberry Daiquiri
From Shari's kitchen

¼ cup dark rum
1 tablespoon strawberry liqueur
1 tablespoon grenadine
1 tablespoon Rose's lime juice
4 strawberries, hulled and coarsely chopped
1 tablespoon sugar
1 whole strawberry for garnish

Combine rum, strawberry liqueur, grenadine, lime juice and chopped strawberries with 2 cups of crushed ice in blender. Blend until smooth.

Wet the rim of a martini glass and dip into sugar. Pour daiquiri into glass and garnish with split strawberry.

Coconut Fruit Smoothies

From Shari's kitchen

½ of 13.5 oz. can Coconut Milk (3/4 cup & 2 tablespoons)
¾ cup orange juice
1 cup ice cubes
½ cup fruit of choice (bananas, berries, mango)
Sugar or honey to taste or 1/3 protein powder

Add coconut milk, orange juice, ice, fruit, sweetener or protein powder to blender. Blend to desired consistency.

Equivalents & Emergency Substitutions

1 whole egg	= ¼ cup egg substitute
1 whole egg	= 2 egg whites
1 whole egg	= 2 egg yolks plus 1 T. water
1 whole egg	= 2 egg yolk (for custards or similar)
1 cup	= 4-6 whole eggs or
	= 8-10 egg whites or
	= 12-14 egg yolks
Baking Powder	= 1 t. cream of tartar plus ¼ t. baking soda
Chocolate, one Square (1 oz. Unsweetened	= 3 T. cocoa plus 1 T. shortening
Cornstarch, 1 T.	= 2 T. all-purpose flour
Garlic, 1 clove	= ¼ t. garlic powder
Honey. 1 cup	= 1 ¼ cup sugar plus ¼ cup liquid
Milk, 1 cup	= ½ c. evap. milk plus ½ c. water
Milk, 1 cup	= 1 c. reconstituted nonfat dry milk Plus 2 T. butter
Sour Milk or Buttermilk, 1 c.	= 1 tsp. lemon juice or vinegar plus Whole milk to make one cup
Onion, ¼ cup	= 1 T. instant minced onion or 1 t. onion powder

About Shari

Shari W. Quinn is the best-selling author of *Disloyalty*, and a NBC's Albany affiliate, WNYT News Channel 13's *Today's Woman.* A native of Albany, New York. After living in suburban Atlanta for eight years, she relocated back to New York's Capital Region. She is a leader in education, a college instructor, and has been in the higher education industry for more than 15 years. She has served as a guest speaker in over 75 high schools throughout New York State.

She earned her Master's degree in Business Administration (MBA) with a concentration in Marketing from the University of Phoenix in Atlanta; a Bachelor's in Marketing and Management from Siena College in Loudonville, New York; and an Associate's degree in Liberal Arts from Hudson Valley Community College in Troy, New York. She has completed more than two years toward her Doctor of Education (Ed.D.) degree in Educational Leadership, and is currently pursuing her doctoral degree with Northeastern University in Boston.

She is the proud mother of three children, Sharia, Ruffus "Pop" IV, and Malik; has two beautiful grandchildren, Anthony Jr., and DeShari'ay; and lives in upstate New York.

About Ann

Ann Johnson, a native of Alabama, recently retired after 38 years with the New York State Division of Children and Family Services. As her first retirement project, she co-authored the cookbook, *Taste!*, as she enjoys cooking, baking and is a collector of recipes.

She attended and graduated from high school in Albany, NY; and always wanted to be a psychologist. She earned her Bachelors of Social Work (BSW) from the State University of New York at Brockport.

Prior to becoming a caseworker, Ann worked with Monroe County (NY) where her first job was with the Children's Detention Center. She later became an Examiner and was promoted to caseworker in the Children and Family Services Division where she held various roles in CPS, Employment and Preventive Day Care. Social work and serving others has always been her passion and she couldn't have imaged working in any other field.

She is the proud mother of the three Ds - Darryl, Derrius and Dedderick. All three of her sons thinks she analyzes too much and tends to *social work* with them. Nonetheless, they ravish in her delicious home cooked meals and are always making special requests.

During retirement, she looks forward to sleeping in, relaxing and enjoying her grandchildren, along with the peace and quiet. Ann currently lives in Rochester, NY.

Diversity Quilt Poem

When I think of
diversity and inclusion
I think of
Grandma's handmade quilt,
a colorful collage
of accepted and respected
set of values, beliefs
and beautiful differences
with a collection of delicate patches,
contrasting fabrics and complex textures,
each telling its own ageless story
carefully stitched and woven together,
using threads of dignity, integrity and humility
to reshape and redirect
our mis-perception
and redefine our perspective
to give a better appreciation and admiration
for the many different people,
ideas, cultures and lifestyles of this world
to add value to our being
depth to our lives
warmth to our soul
all without seeing color
in the timeless masterpiece
of grandma's handmade quilt.